Fundamentals of Strategy:
The Legacy of Henry Eccles

Scott A. Boorman

The BiblioGov Project is an effort to expand awareness of the public documents and records of the U.S. Government via print publications. In broadening the public understanding of government and its work, an enlightened democracy can grow and prosper. Ranging from historic Congressional Bills to the most recent Budget of the United States Government, the BiblioGov Project spans a wealth of government information. These works are now made available through an environmentally friendly, print-on-demand basis, using only what is necessary to meet the required demands of an interested public. We invite you to learn of the records of the U.S. Government, heightening the knowledge and debate that can lead from such publications.

Included are the following Collections:

Budget of The United States Government
Presidential Documents
United States Code
Education Reports from ERIC
GAO Reports
History of Bills
House Rules and Manual
Public and Private Laws

Code of Federal Regulations
Congressional Documents
Economic Indicators
Federal Register
Government Manuals
House Journal
Privacy act Issuances
Statutes at Large

FUNDAMENTALS OF STRATEGY
The Legacy of Henry Eccles

Scott A. Boorman

M any people have valuable insights regarding strategy. Much less wide-spread is a capability of generating fresh and important analytical insights at will or on command as new strategic situations and problems arise.

Here we aim to capture the active ingredients of precisely such a capability that took shape at the Naval War College shortly after World War II. Emanating from efforts of the Spruance-era College to integrate analytically, and to codify for the benefit of the United States in future conflicts, lessons learned from U.S. military successes in the Pacific in a time of maximum naval effort, this body of analytical thought and writing is exceedingly valuable. While much has changed, many of the most basic realities of how logistics permeates strategy remain as true now as then. Because this military and intellectual legacy is now at risk of being imperfectly remembered, when it is remembered at all, this article also aims to bring to current attention some important early post–World War II Naval War College writing on strategy.

The leader in these steps to codify relevant military lessons was then-Captain Henry E. Eccles, USN (he retired in 1952 as a rear admiral).[1] Starting during the Naval War College presidency of Admiral Raymond A. Spruance—victor of many Pacific War operations, culminating in the Okinawa campaign—Eccles served as founding head (1947–51) of the Department of Logistics (later renamed Department of Strategy and Logistics) at the College.[2] In part reflecting strands of Eccles's World War II experience in the Pacific, where he was eventually charged with planning

Scott A. Boorman is professor of sociology, Department of Sociology, Yale University. He received his PhD from Harvard and JD from the Yale Law School. Besides military and logistics analysis in the tradition of Admiral Eccles, his research interests include mathematical models of social structure and processes, network analysis, effects of information technology, complex statutes, and complex organizations.

© 2009 by Scott A. Boorman
Naval War College Review, Spring 2009, Vol. 62, No. 2

coordination of all bases of all U.S. armed services for the planned invasion of Japan (projected to involve up to five million American military personnel), Eccles's written analytical work on war and logistics has a notably systematic quality and an eye for structural issues.[3] Eccles served at the heart of the Pacific War U.S. naval effort, one of the major success stories in world military history, and he knew in an unfiltered way the ingredients that made that success possible; the distinction between the militarily vital, the important, and the merely desirable; what is military reality versus arrows on a map or word pictures in smooth language. He had the insight, motivation, and tenacity to put this knowledge down on paper—in the blunt, unvarnished language of U.S. naval officers of his era, using few acronyms and without civilian jargon.

This work initially took shape in the form of numerous unpublished documents circulated in the Navy and beyond, augmented by extensive correspondence. Eventually, this military thought began to appear in journal articles and books by Eccles.[4] Supplemented at points by comments noting applications of Eccles's insights to twenty-first-century contexts, this article builds on research with the Eccles Papers held in the Naval Historical Collection at the Naval War College.[5]

Two key observations—one substantive, one methodological—anchor and orient the present inquiry. The first is that strategy, in both theory and practice, is permeated and shaped by three sets of forces: logistical, psychological (particularly centering on the psychological aspects of command), and bureaucratic.[6] In modern war each of these forces is always present and always important. Something of the complexity of the exercise of modern high command is suggested by the fact that the three sets of forces, viewed in dynamic systems terms, exhibit very different operating characteristics yet coexist (often in tightly coupled ways) in the concrete conflict situations that commanders must navigate.

The second observation is more Clausewitzian: while the application of strategic principles to particular situations is infinitely variable and at times subtle, the fundamentals of strategy are *relatively* few and simple. This means that it is feasible to create a concise but carefully structured statement of these fundamentals that can be drawn on as a conceptual aid, or template, to help craft strategic approaches as current strategic conditions mutate and fundamentally new situations arise.[7]

Inevitably such a template of theory can reach only so far, and its central use is creation of a sound starting point that more detailed analysis should develop further in any given concrete context. Inevitably too, practical use of theory can never be fully mechanized, and there is always a key element of interpretation—and therefore of intellectual craftsmanship—in moving from theory to application.

The analytical discussion below is structured in three parts. The first is a definition (or description) of the concept of strategy. The second places strategy in a larger context (an analytical activity that may also be conceived as exploring pertinent "boundary conditions" that shape strategy). The third elaborates, subject to space constraints in this article, upon three specific interlocking themes: logistics, control, and flexibility. This third part is particularly conceived in the spirit of helping strategists ask good questions and generate creative strategic ideas. It is not intended to illuminate all dimensions of this many-dimensional subject.

For analytic focus, our emphasis is primarily (though not exclusively) on political-military affairs, which are the traditional heart of strategic studies—though in an ever more complex and civilianized world it is increasingly clear that many twenty-first-century growing points of strategic theory and practice will bear little surface resemblance to twentieth-century war. Here again the legacy of the early post–World War II Naval War College shows its tough intellectual fiber to advantage, since the tripartite emphasis on approaching strategy from the perspectives of logistics, command psychology, and bureaucracy that took shape in that era is well suited to encouraging clear thinking about the conflict environments of the century we are now in.

WHAT STRATEGY IS

The roots of the present analysis lie in a terse memorandum, one of the best short writings on strategy ever penned, written in 1955 by Herbert Rosinski, a Nazi-era émigré German historian.[8] Central to this document is its theme of "strategy as control," which (as importantly further developed by Eccles with an eye to logistics) may be stated in shorthand form as follows:[9]

> Strategy = the *comprehensive direction* of *power* to *control situations and areas* to *attain broad objectives.*

Given the game-theoretic focus that nowadays so often structures the discussion of issues deemed "strategic," it is important to note that the concept of strategy advanced here is essentially a substantive, *not* a mathematical, one.[10] This is as it should be, since actual strategic problems are typically far too complex to be reliably reduced to any single formalism. It is also important that the definition of strategy just given also combines well with further definitions of tactics and logistics.[11]

Each element of this definition—comprising the seven words or phrases listed below—deserves careful scrutiny and exegesis. It is useful to be alert to ways in which a particular word or phrase can be *mis*used or *mis*understood—thus illuminating roots of strategic *error* (a rich area for strategic analysis whose crucial importance Clausewitz intuitively grasped and that much game theory tends to ignore or deemphasize).

Comprehensive orients one toward framing strategic calculation as broadly as possible, missing no "level." It is remarkable how often intelligent, educated people fail to grasp this and by so doing fall short of thinking strategically. Elaborating on "comprehensive" points to three broad classes of problems facing a strategist:[12]

- *Control of the external field of action,* whose central focus is the adversary or adversaries (but may also be expanded to include allies and neutrals).

- *Control of the internal field of action,* whose focus is the roots of power on which the strategist draws (e.g., political, public opinion, producer logistics, industrial base, and other "upstream" sources of power, at times extending to the family and social network of a leader or commander).

- *Control of the means of control.* In the modern era, such means widely pivot on the general staffs used to surmount cognitive and physical limitations on any commander, but also come to involve other bureaucracies, complex organizations, and social networks, many outside the traditional "defense establishment."[13] Control of the means of control is far more complex than it first appears, too commonly draining the creativity crucially needed for the other two problems. Twentieth-century experience suggests two basic insights: first, that there is a powerful dynamic by which machinery to exert such control tends to become ever more elaborate, so that its use requires more learning time and attention from commanders;[14] second, that such machinery is a breeding ground for organizational failures, perhaps multiple, at times of low visibility.[15]

Direction involves the standard sorts of "s/he thinks I think s/he thinks" calculations widely associated with "thinking strategically" in a world attuned to modern game theory. It *also* involves many other things, including (for example) less glamorous but exceedingly crucial logistics calculations as well as active use of diplomatic skill sets to navigate the outer boundaries of the authority a commander wields.

Power needs to be given very broad scope, subsuming many different species of power, military and civilian alike. The complexity of twenty-first-century societies invites imaginative identification of new species of power. Because of the universal dependence on some form of logistics support, the exercise of power in practice is often much more complex and more decentralized than is power in theory—which means that it is often productive to analyze particular types of power through the prism of their logistics requirements.[16]

In strategic environments where certain types of power are "off the table" at a given time (i.e., are not effectively usable to achieve given political ends), a basic challenge for strategists is developing intuition for when a particular type of power has moved, or is about to move, from an "effectively unusable" to an "effectively usable" category (or vice versa).[17] Note that the dynamics here, centering around qualitative change in a conflict situation, are frequently more psychological and at times bureaucratic than technical and accordingly may easily elude analyses based on rational-choice assumptions—with a concomitant potential for strategic surprise, such as when foes come from very different cultures.

Control—and focus on its implications and ramifications—is the active ingredient of Rosinski's seminal 1955 contribution; as control's antithesis he points to a "haphazard series of improvisations." Importantly, control is also a highly developed engineering concept, a fact that can be used to facilitate conveying strategic ideas to military officers and relevant civilians whose professional roots often lie in engineering and allied areas. One key advantage of conceptualizing "strategy as control" is the way it invites—as not all concepts of "strategy" do—exploration of a natural agenda of questions concerning temporal and other parameters of control (see below). In fact, the control that a strategist is able to exert often amounts to little more than a "patch" on more basic ongoing dynamics—for instance, political, economic, demographic, epidemiological.

The phrase *situations and areas* represents the contexts within which control is sought. Note that the present definition of strategy steps beyond the geopolitical, often deeply territorial focus of the world wars and much other warfare, giving flexibility to subsume, say, bureaucratic warfare, "inner court" factional politics, and other frequently bitter and protracted, yet *not* territorial, struggles.

Attaining objectives raises the challenge of defining the criteria of judgment underlying this concept—and in a surprising array of strategic problems such criteria are notably unclear.

Objectives refers to actual, not declaratory, strategy. In a world where public relations has become a function of command often no less important than the classic duties of a general staff, it is all too easy for strategists to let their declaratory strategies edit their real goals. In one limiting case of this kind of error, the "objective" is replaced by a mere slogan—which may be accepted with little analysis within an inner circle of high command as well as circulated among a wider public. High-level decision makers in totalitarian (and some authoritarian) societies may be particularly prone to this sort of pitfall, sometimes opening exploitable vulnerabilities because their decision support structures explicitly lack the traditions of "airing" of alternative positions on issues and general intellectual openness historically associated with the Naval War College.[18]

An interesting and increasingly important variant problem may arise when a mission statement is frozen into statute, with all the legal ramifications that brings with it.

The antidote for such pitfalls starts with sound, careful, even plodding *analysis* of actual strategic objectives—that is, clarification of what the strategist truly must accomplish. Breadth of objectives, however—which is one of the true hallmarks of strategy, by contrast to tactics (a distinction game theory characteristically elides)—means that such analysis is rarely trivial, precisely because broad goals are typically intangible, at times highly abstract, and therefore elusive. To this problem of analysis, which lies at the heart of strategic tasks, we return shortly.

STRATEGY IN A LARGER CONTEXT

There are three ways in which a larger context imposes structure on strategy and strategic planning.

Strategic Objectives and Their Analysis

The purest form of strategic labor is the analysis of objectives. Although not sufficient by itself, the first (and often psychologically difficult) step in effective analysis of this sort in concrete situations is recognizing that here lies a challenging, often deep, problem—one that certainly outstrips the capabilities of any single formal or other "model."

Concepts like "victory" and "defeat" (or indeed "war" and "peace") are commonly of little help in analyzing objectives. The difficulty of this task (compounded if a strategic situation is rapidly changing) may be greatly magnified by potent psychological and bureaucratic forces contributing to what is sometimes known as "goal displacement."[19] Additional factors may also frustrate clear analysis of objectives. For example, *too* clear an analysis may tend to undermine the roots of a strategist's authority—or the glue that holds together a coalition.[20]

The task of analyzing objectives is frequently elided or otherwise underestimated by the intellectual traditions of "rational choice," which widely posit that objectives or their functional equivalents and proxies (e.g., payoff values assigned to game outcomes) have already been effectively analyzed and may therefore simply be treated as known parameters.[21]

With the crucial proviso that strategy must always remain dominant—logistics exists to serve strategy, *never* the other way around—logistics analysis must always accompany the strategic imagination. Such analysis includes continually probing the boundary between what is logistically feasible and what is not, and other logistics ramifications of strategic objectives. Logistics analysis may at times advise changes of goals—because of logistics limitations on one's own side or an adversary's exploitable logistics weaknesses. It should also be borne in mind that logistics (from well functioning supply chains to the health of the population) is the engine of the better peace that is the ultimate aim of most wars—and that engine requires analysis, not just after the war but during it.

Language and semantic analysis have roles to play too.[22] Part of the task in analyzing strategic objectives is to ferret out conceptual failures—because hazily envisioned future events are the focus—lurking beneath the smooth language in which polished statements of high-level strategic objectives are so often framed.[23]

Because quantification in high-level strategic matters commonly has limited meaning or utility, as a practical matter the analysis of objectives commonly involves devising a hierarchy of qualitative goals, conjoined with a timetable for their accomplishment. It is worth bearing in mind that there are many instances, worldwide, where high-level strategies—and decisions highly relevant to U.S. national interests—emanate from people who are not professional soldiers, who may literally never have heard of a U.S. military operation order, and whose approaches to objectives differ fundamentally from those of the U.S. military.[24]

Relationship between Strategy and the Type of War Being Fought

This is the second genuinely deep problem facing the strategist:[25] correctly analyzing the social, political, and other dynamics that form the larger context of

FOUR FUNDAMENTAL STRUCTURES: SELECTED RESEARCH FOCI

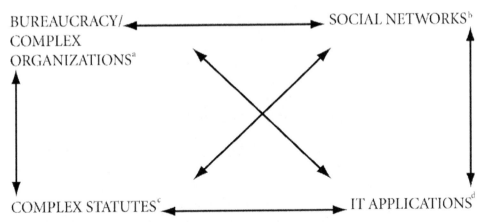

Notes:
a. Formal organizational tables of organization, plus command, control, and communications.
b. Multiple types of interlocking networks.
c. Shorthand for complex doctrine in a legal-administrative sense.
d. Information technology (IT)—including algorithms, software, computer networks, and implementation.

These structures, each a component of the twenty-first-century landscape presenting formidable control challenges, are marked by massive and growing complexity; are distinct but ever more interlocked; are new in significant aspects (symbolized by the bidirectional arrows); often have major but inconspicuous impacts; and require analysis, singly and in combination.

war and peace, with an eye to identifying opportunities to piggyback strategic control on more basic structural patterns and trends. More than an intelligence problem, this is a task for broad and creative social observation and analysis, commonly requiring a mix of qualitative and quantitative strands.[26]

In a related spirit, the figure aims to help break strategists' attentions out of the grip of standard emphases in the lion's share of twentieth-century writings on war and strategy, focusing instead on analyzing four fundamental structures that will, singly and jointly, do much to shape twenty-first-century conflict environments. Deleting any vertex in this figure, or collapsing any two vertices, risks significant analytical distortion, because the operating characteristics of each type of structure are different from those of the other ones.

In a world where markets with prices rule, an important Eccles caution merits restating: the ability to carry out the relevant analysis effectively is "a rare intellectual quality that cannot be made to order or purchased on the open market."[27] Failure in this task of analysis portends perhaps the greatest *controllable* pitfall facing any strategist—that of attempting to operate strategically in an imaginary world!

A crucial strand of the analytic problem here lies in recognizing what Martin Shubik has termed the "games within the game." These are subsidiary games involving often extraneous political purposes whose existence greatly complicates the main "game" in which the strategist is centrally involved, giving lasting, nontrivial meaning to Clausewitz's fundamental insistence on the primacy of war's political purpose.[28]

Roots of Strategy in National or Other Human Values

The third deep way in which larger context impinges on the strategist is the need to craft strategy to be in harmony with the fundamental values of the larger collectivity (nation, party, faction, or other) that the strategist serves. Such values may include that collectivity's concepts of victory and defeat, its affinity with certain weapons or tools of conflict, and its affinity with certain overall styles of conflict (e.g., short war versus protracted war, positional versus mobile versus guerrilla warfare). Harmony with such fundamental, often tacit, values can be a vast source of strategic strength. In some ways, such harmony is akin to an intangible logistics reserve—a reserve of strategic poise and stamina. In the World War II era, U.S. strategy achieved and sustained notable harmony with fundamental values and aspirations of the American people. In Vietnam, there was enormous—and ultimately insuperable—friction between the personal values and goals of a large segment of the American population and war aims in a protracted land war in Asia.[29]

Of course, value harmonization issues face adversaries no less than one's own side. This fact creates an enduring niche for analysis geared to recognizing often subtle strategic opportunities arising when an adversary's course of action starts to veer away from his fundamental values, with concomitant potential for exploitable adversary mistakes. Recognizing this kind of opportunity requires special alertness to pitfalls of "mirror imaging" often born of bureaucracy.

IN SEARCH OF PRINCIPLES OF STRATEGY

What follows is an Eccles-inspired line of inquiry for orienting and structuring a particular strategic analysis project. The central themes of this line of inquiry—logistics, control, flexibility—may also be interpreted as "probes" into principles of strategy.[30] Inevitably, given present space constraints, each basic point below can be raised only briefly and may require imaginative analogical thinking—or a translator's instincts—if full benefit is to be derived in application to twenty-first-century conflict situations very different from World War II.

Advanced-base development work, where a major part of Eccles's World War II experience lay, was a distinctive and in many ways nontraditional brand of logistics—one marked by an integrative viewpoint spanning many functional logistics specialties while looking simultaneously forward to combat areas and back across the Pacific to the continental United States.[31] This viewpoint, in which long-haul transportation issues held center stage and underlined key differences between short- and long-range amphibious operations, did much to shape Eccles's larger view of the logistics process in relation to strategy. As was thoroughly appreciated by Eccles and other analysts at the early post–World War II Naval War College, logistics in modern warfare is inherently a sophisticated concept with important pure and applied, as well as command and technical, levels.[32]

Many of the logistics insights of the World War II era that Eccles codified have been thoroughly assimilated and institutionalized by the U.S. military. Yet areas of structural tension and debate persist, and some trade-offs defy permanent resolution.[33] To shed light on such issues, logistics lessons learned from U.S. World War II success must be constantly restudied, restated, and retaught—in ways, one hopes, that attract genuine interest, animated by a sense of curiosity, from broad audiences of U.S. military officers plus relevant civilians. Application of the same basic lessons remains significantly less well incorporated in U.S. logistics capabilities for supporting strategic action of nonmilitary types (among them, capabilities for "nation building"). Meanwhile, a third application of those lessons pertains to Liddell Hart's "the other side of the hill"—i.e., the situation of the adversary. U.S. adversaries have often *not* learned how to do some basic part of their logistics quite right, so that a further strand of the living legacy of Admiral Eccles is to suggest ways of identifying and exploiting resulting vulnerabilities.

For working purposes here, logistics—following Eccles—may be defined as the creation and sustained support of weapons and forces to be tactically employed to attain strategic objectives. Yet more simply: "Logistics is the means of war."[34]

In the background of this description lies the concept that *logistics is a dynamic system,* one whose operating characteristics are a rich source of principles closely related to, yet not the same as, directly strategic principles, specifically including those familiar from the rubric of the "principles of war."[35] In modern warfare, this dynamic system is heavily implemented through an enormously complex defense bureaucracy, yet it has an identity that is not simply reducible to such bureaucracy. While logistics is closely related to economics, the logistics process also importantly operates in many nonmarket contexts—including, of course, combat environments. For related reasons, logistics analysis is not reducible to, even though it obviously overlaps with, standard economic analysis. Logistics processes have important psychological dimensions (e.g., Eccles emphasized the role of social trust in the provision of logistics support in combat or other wartime conditions).[36] Such psychological aspects of logistics often coexist awkwardly with standard rational-choice models of the sort that most economists favor.

Logistics permeates military effort, and in many military contexts the true contest, extending to both war and peace, is as much between two logistics systems as between two sets of tactical organizations (indeed, it is possible to parse the Cold War from this viewpoint). To appreciate the true force of this point, it is important to recognize that logistics factors and principles continue to operate—often with enormously potent effects—whatever those factors and principles may be called. Military terminology is often driven by bureaucratic "chop lines" and other organizational compromises, so that much logistics structure and process in modern warfare appear in other guises. Components of a military establishment that are actually designated as "logistics" organizations are therefore frequently pale reflections of the true magnitude of the logistics process.[37]

Building on this background, what follows may be treated as a candidate for the "first principle of strategic logistics."[38]

In modern war, logistics is the soft underbelly of combat power, vastly more vulnerable to effective attack—at times direct and obvious, at times indirect and low-visibility—than is the combat power itself. Underscoring this proposition is the enormous sweep of logistics activities, ranging over supply, transportation, base development, weapons systems support, maintenance and repair, personnel, and medical and public health functions. Exploiting the consequences of the adversary's logistics dependence, while defending against logistics depredations by an alert, aggressive foe, is therefore a pivotal ingredient of modern strategy as well as a fine illustration of the strategic necessity of a comprehensive perspective that ranges far beyond standard combat operations.

Post–World War II analyses suggest that the Japanese missed many opportunities to attack the complicated and often fragile logistics on which U.S. offensives in the Pacific depended.[39] From that day to this it is not obvious that the United States has *ever* faced a major adversary who has pushed as hard and as imaginatively as possible to attack the logistics system on which U.S. military strength depends. There exist strands of relevant U.S. military experience (e.g., Iraqi Scud missile attack on the port city of Al Jubayl, Saudi Arabia, during Operation DESERT STORM);[40] nonetheless, the nation may remain in some ways an *in*experienced superpower in "logistics war."[41]

By extension (although the terminology used is often different), logistics is also a major source of vulnerability in nonmilitary types of conflict, with the high connectivity and fragility of civilian society affording a combinatorial explosion of logistics targets. U.S. vulnerabilities to sabotage—including its more subtle forms, such as "slow-down or misdirection of effort in certain key industries"—particularly caught Eccles's attention during his years as head of the Naval War College Logistics Department.[42]

But the dependence of strategy on logistics has further—and in some ways yet more far-reaching and challenging—ramifications. Perhaps surprisingly for some audiences, the heart of Eccles's logistics thought, as documented by careful reading of the Eccles Papers, actually points is a somewhat different direction from that just explored.

Specifically, in much of modern warfare the most important (and difficult) "game" confronting a commander may be that associated with the struggle to assert command and control over his own logistics (a struggle on which any adverse effects of hostile action are an overlay).[43] Central here is the principle of the "logistics snowball," which in Eccles's classic formulation describes the tendency of the logistics support of combat power to grow to a size out of all proportion to that of the combat forces supported—until, like a snowball being pushed up a hill, logistics becomes so massive and sluggish that further progress is barely possible.[44]

This is a fundamental insight into how logistics systems behave as dynamic systems, as true in the twenty-first century as in the World War II era.[45] Major contemporary versions and generalizations of the "snowball" effect and its ramifications may be found in many of the structures on which twenty-first-century societies rest (see again the figure on page 97): bureaucracy and complex organizations; social networks (comprising multiple types of network ties);

algorithms, software, and computer networks; and complex statutes and administrative regulations—among them, procurement regulations.

To the extent that taming the snowball is not an impossible game, the feasibility of doing so crucially depends on application for strategic purposes of a further set of fundamental principles centering on command and control of the logistics process.[46] Here it is important that under peacetime conditions logistics responsibilities tend to become diffuse.[47] This means that when war or other crises come, the "game" of taming relevant snowball(s) may easily have *no* outcome consistent with achieving a larger strategic purpose within the finite time window allowed by such external forces as public opinion.[48]

Under twenty-first-century conditions this may be an exceptionally important principle, applicable to future uses of power by the United States. To anchor this problem in recent U.S. military experience in Iraq, consider a question posed by Secretary of Defense Robert M. Gates in his 29 September 2008 speech to a National Defense University audience: "Why did we have to go outside the normal bureaucratic process to develop counter-IED [improvised explosive device] technologies, to build MRAPs [mine resistant ambush protected vehicles], and to quickly expand our ISR [intelligence, surveillance, and reconnaissance] capability?"[49]

The difficulty (and urgency) of controlling the logistics snowball naturally begets a further principle: especially given the ultrahigh dimensionality of modern logistics, dependence of strategy on logistics also gives ample room for updated and expanded versions of the old saying "He who controls the spare parts controls the operation."

With the caveat that strategy must always remain dominant, enough has been said to suggest a further principle: At sufficiently high levels of command—and perhaps separately, at sufficiently deep levels of analysis—strategy and logistics tend to coalesce.[50]

Strategy-as-control is *not* about making no mistakes. The cold, pale light of logistics reality alone makes this virtually impossible. Success tends to go to the side that makes the fewest mistakes, or at any rate the fewest major ones. "Control" is, in short, often a highly imperfect construct—a point that many devotees of mathematics in strategic analysis tend to miss.

One reason the strategy-as-control theme is so productive as a launching point for the development of strategic principles is that it invites a range of searching analytic questions in any given strategic context (consider, e.g., a context involving potential use of biological weapons or of weapons whose use has long-term environmental implications).

One useful specific list of such questions appears in Eccles's writings on strategy.[51] This list follows (and note that the more seriously any of the questions on it is pursued, the more logistics issues tend to arise):

What to control [i.e., the object or objects of control; and note here that
strategy-as-control is commonly cumulative],

What is the purpose of this control,

What is the nature of the control,

What degree of control is necessary,

When the control is to be initiated,

How long the control is to be maintained,

What general method or scheme of control is to be used.

Perhaps most fundamentally, strategy-as-control clarifies the essential unity
of its subject matter across diverse spheres of human action. At the same time,
the concept also encourages analysis of interesting special cases—for example,
control directed at the self.[52]

Grand strategy may be interpreted as a special case where either: (1) control is
sought with a distinctively deep time horizon (e.g., as in "grand strategy of the
Chinese empire");[53] or (2) the search for such control has a distinctively combinatorial aspect, bringing into play a mix of tools of many kinds—among them,
diplomatic, psychological, and economic, as well as purely military.[54] The sheer
multiplicity of types of networks simultaneously in play in many twenty-
first-century conflicts is compelling more conflict actors than ever before—many of them nongovernmental—to attempt to think and operate as
grand strategists in sense (2). As the long twentieth-century century road to
building U.S. joint operations capability suggests by partial analogy,[55] actually
achieving the integration of tools grand strategy requires is far from easy.[56] Indeed,
such integration is in many ways harder than that involved in military joint operations, since nonmilitary tools are so diverse—often relative to each other no less
than to military ones—and are intertwined with comparably diverse organizations, logistics, and even basic assumptions about human nature and society.[57]

Even beneath a level of grand strategy, the strategy-as-control theme valuably
deflects focus from any one tool or weapon of conflict (which, pushed to a logi-
cal limit, produces the pathology Eccles dubbed "weapon strategy"), instead expanding attention given to integrated employment of *all* available tools in
generating the desired extent and nature of control. Because so many military
officers and relevant civilian professionals have career backgrounds heavily in-
vested in specific weapons systems, a strategy-as-control viewpoint can do valuable service in helping avert incipient "weapon strategy" traps.[58] Here again it is
relevant to note that strategy-as-control connects on a basic level with themes of
control central to modern engineering theory and practice (note, for example,
the crucial importance of time and timing factors in strategy). A particularly

important strand of the strategy-as-control theme—one that will be of fundamental importance in many twenty-first-century contexts—is its profound connection with a world of ever deeper dependence on software and the mathematical-logical algorithms that software embodies.[59]

One major contrast case for strategy-as-control is "strategy as destruction," a false equation that received much currency early in the nuclear age.[60] This false equation finds more recent reflection in widespread tacit assumptions that biological or chemical attacks are necessarily geared to creating maximum feasible destructive impact on a human group, as contrasted with more nuanced manipulations of political and social processes in target societies.[61]

Strategy-as-control is also a fine starting point for capturing, comparing, and transposing the active ingredients of some of the most distinguished contributions to strategic thought spanning many cultures and historical eras. Among these are (moving roughly from east to west): Chinese (here note not only Sun Tzu and the Chinese military tradition but also lessons born of two millenniums of imperial Chinese bureaucracy), Mongol, Indian subcontinent, Iranian (e.g., note mirrors-of-princes advice literature), Arab, Ottoman, and Byzantine. In some cases non-Western strategic and other intellectual traditions may contain important insights about control possibilities that are little known or developed in Western contexts.[62]

A focus on strategy-as-control leads naturally to a focus on strategic flexibility and its roots. In some contexts, strategy certainly demands decisive action or some extremely carefully reasoned form of irreversible commitment of the sort analyzed in the strategic writings of Thomas Schelling.[63] Yet the fog of war, fluidity of long-term situations, and ultimately the opacity of complex social structure and process itself (perhaps the richest of all sources of uncertainty facing a strategist) guarantee that strategic flexibility needs to be available when desired—as it often will be.

In thinking about the roots of flexibility, or deficit thereof, it is helpful to distinguish two quite different classes of contributing factors, each having many strands. In this regard, note also a basic asymmetry: producing strategic flexibility typically requires many ingredients, but inducing strategic *in*flexibility may need only one.

The first set of factors centers around the mind of command and is essentially psychological (or sociological, if one allows for the role of staff and others in the commander's environment, often amounting to a well defined social structure). Psychological flexibility may be easy to attain in theory, but (as Clausewitz saw clearly long ago) it is vastly harder amid the stunning emotional and physical pressures of bitter conflict with deadly force. In particular, circumstances may require juggling denial of the possibility of failure of strategic *ends*—even where all evidence is to the contrary—while at the same time exhibiting the highest level of virtuosity in shifting with poise and flexibility among choices of *means*. Such pressures may be short-term (say, hours or days), or they may be long-term (such as protracted revolutionary war), with quite different psychological contexts and consequences.

In addition, more subtle forms of flexibility loss, amounting to creeping institutional inertia, may accumulate as a largely unplanned by-product of the operation of institutions of command over a long period of time—via persistence of flawed decisions that many recognize as flawed yet that no one seems to know how to correct (even when, at times, those decisions far outlast the organizational tenure of those who made them). As institutions of command, including bureaucracies, age through the course of the twenty-first century, these subtle institutional flaws and the loss of strategic flexibility they entail may become more pronounced.

The second set of factors returns to logistics and centers around the physical substance of flexibility—the quality of a strategist's logistics, especially transportation. One of the twentieth century's most powerful examples of logistics flexibility as foundation of strategic flexibility is the relationship between the success in World War II of U.S. naval operations in the Pacific and the wartime development of mobile logistics support and the strategic mobility it permitted. It is well worth reflecting on the quality of logistics thought and leadership that made such innovation possible midstream in a great war.[64]

THE DUALITY OF STRATEGIC AND LOGISTICS ANALYSIS

Crafting high-level strategy is, and will remain, extraordinarily difficult. This is because logistics, psychology, and bureaucracy are difficult, often counterintuitive subjects—and few experiences (certainly in ordinary civilian life) adequately prepare anyone to cope at a high level with their interacting complexities. Even individuals who have been outstanding strategists in one strategic context may easily reemerge as blunderers in a different one.[65]

Responding to these challenges, the analytic capability that took shape at the Naval War College in the early post–World War II period was an unusual synthesis—in some ways without precedent—and an enduring U.S. national resource that merits careful continuing study, with an eye both to its substance and to the institutional and intellectual conditions that made such synthesis possible. Although there were numerous strands in the synthesis, at its heart lay the duality of strategic and logistics analysis.[66] Without the strategic level—whose principles this article has sought to retrieve and develop in updated form—logistics tends to unravel into a formless sprawl of technical areas, lacking clear focus and identity. Without constant reference to the logistics foundation, strategic analysis tends to become like much modern art—perhaps intellectually stimulating but of unclear relation to the world as we know it.

With an eye to future applications of the key ideas, the body of theory and principle developed in the present article is geared to three distinct, if related, sets of tasks:[67]

- *Education for modern high command,* centering around inculcating intuitive awareness of the natures and relationships of structural elements of the *full* strategic problem the strategist must be prepared to tackle.

- Creation of a *basic and lasting intellectual organization for the study of strategy,* one that can serve as a "template" for the ongoing development of strategic topics and disciplined accumulation of strategic ideas—thus creating a reserve of strategic and related logistics thinking that can be readily retrieved and consulted under often far-from-ideal crisis conditions, as well as helping with strategic planning more broadly.

- Creation of a *conceptual environment conducive to disciplined forms of strategic creativity,* an environment whose hallmark is fundamentally original, valid, and valuable insights.[68]

While each generation must revisit these tasks with fresh eyes, there are few better starting points for their successful accomplishment than active institutional memory of the pioneering analytic contributions of the U.S. Naval War College in the age of Admirals Raymond A. Spruance and Henry E. Eccles.

NOTES

The author would like to thank, for their comments on earlier versions of this article, Professors Kenneth J. Arrow, Howard L. Boorman, and Sir Michael Howard. For his sustained interest in the substance, as well as invaluable editorial advice, special thanks are owing to Frank Uhlig, Jr. In addition, thanks are also owing to the Naval War College Naval Historical Collection and Dr. Evelyn M. Cherpak, the curator there, as well as to the trustees of the Liddell Hart Centre for Military Archives, King's College London, and the Liddell Hart Centre staff, directed by Patricia Methven. Any errors of fact or interpretation are the author's responsibility alone.

1. For further background on Eccles's career contributions as a U.S. Navy line officer (Naval Academy '22)—emphasizing Eccles's Navy Cross–winning command in combat in the vicinity of Java early in World War II—see the tribute to Eccles by Rear Adm. R. F. Marryott, USN, "President's Notes," *Naval War College Review* 39, no. 4 (Autumn 1986), pp. 4–5. In June 1985 the library of the U.S. Naval War College was named in Admiral Eccles's honor. See Admiral Eccles's "Remarks at Dedication of Eccles Library at Naval War College," *Naval War College Review* 38, no. 6 (November–December 1985), pp. 96–97.

2. The story of the founding of the Naval War College Department of Logistics is told in John B. Hattendorf, B. Mitchell Simpson III, and John R. Wadleigh, *Sailors and Scholars: The Centennial History of the U.S. Naval War College* (Newport, R.I.: Naval War College

Press, 1984), p. 186. On Spruance see Cdr. Thomas B. Buell, USN, *The Quiet Warrior: A Biography of Admiral Raymond A. Spruance* (Boston: Little, Brown, 1974).

3. Within worldwide traditions of military and related strategic theory—holding aside the game-theoretic tradition—the major theorists besides Eccles whose analytical work exhibits comparably systematic and codifying instincts are Napoleon's two leading interpreters, Clausewitz and Jomini. In effect, Eccles's writings are placeholders for "thoughts on war" of a major part of the World War II generation of senior U.S. Navy leaders. Of course, full consensus across a population of strong-minded professionals can never be expected—a point on which Eccles, for one, was thoroughly realistic. (To illustrate, a specific conceptual disagreement in Naval War College circles on the relation of logistics to strategy is noted by Eccles, "Logistics and Strategy," *Naval War College Review* 10, no. 5 [January 1958], p. 25.)

4. Eccles's books were *Operational Naval Logistics,* NAVPERS 10869 (Washington, D.C.: Bureau of Naval Personnel, April 1950); *Logistics in the National Defense,* 1st ed. (Harrisburg, Pa.: Stackpole, 1959); *Military Concepts and Philosophy* (New Brunswick, N.J.: Rutgers Univ. Press, 1965); and *Military Power in a Free Society* (Newport, R.I.: Naval War College Press, 1979). Both the 1959 and the 1965 books were written with support from the Office of Naval Research (ONR) through the George Washington University Logistics Research Project. A further sampler of Eccles's published writings, augmented by the limited but important set of his unpublished writings represented in the Naval War College Library catalog, appears in *Naval War College Review* 30, no. 1 (Summer 1977), pp. 26–27. This list is usefully supplemented by a list of Eccles's publications in the *Naval War College Review*, contained in the *Review* index (available online or on compact disc); most, but not all, signed Eccles publications in the *Review* appear on this list. In its "Author" section this index—providing a profile of a major U.S. military periodical published continuously since its founding in 1948—contains more single-authored entries under Eccles's name than under that of any other individual author.

5. The Eccles Papers Project, which was initiated in 1986 at Admiral Eccles's request and invitation to the present author and Dr. Paul R. Levitt (a mathematician who died in 1999), is announced and briefly described in U.S. Naval Academy Alumni Association *Shipmate* 49, no. 9 (November 1986), p. 13. Hereafter the notation "EP *X.Y*" refers to box *X*, folder *Y* in the Eccles Papers in the Naval War College Naval Historical Collection.

6. Two key Eccles observations help give unity to these three topics of logistics, command psychology, and bureaucracy. The first is that the modern logistics organization is the home of *complex organization;* see, for example, comment in *Operational Naval Logistics,* p. 29, to the effect that logistics organizations tend to be much more complex than tactical ones. In many ways *Operational Naval Logistics* is a book about bureaucracy. The second observation is that the perspective of command by its nature must reconcile conflicting imperatives of strategy, logistics, and tactics—a task that involves many psychological as well as bureaucratic challenges. The interconnectedness of strategy, logistics, and tactics is symbolized by the interlocking-rings diagram in Eccles, "Theatre Logistic Planning," *U.S. Naval War College Information Service for Officers* 3, no. 2 (October 1950), p. 3. (This was the predecessor publication to the *Naval War College Review.*)

7. Related "template making" instincts are already plainly apparent in Eccles's "Basic Elements and Aspects of Logistics," 27 August 1947, typescript of his lecture launching the first year of the Naval War College Logistics Course (EP 30.21). In much more highly developed form, Eccles's structural approach to modern warfare is presented in his *Command Logistics,* submitted with foreword dated 8 February 1956 by Capt. K. E. Jung, USN, Head, Strategy and Logistics Dept., and approved by Rear Adm. Thomas H. Robbins, Jr., USN, Chief of Staff (Newport, R.I.: Naval War College, 1956) (EP 44.3, copy identified as "Issue to Naval Warfare Class, 1956"; also held in the Eccles Library of the Naval War College).

8. See Eccles, *Military Concepts and Philosophy,* p. 313 note 4, identifying this memo, "New Thoughts on Strategy," as "written by Dr. Herbert Rosinski in September, 1955,

following informal discussions with the President of the Naval War College, Vice Admiral Lynde McCormick, and his chief of staff, Rear Admiral Thomas H. Robbins, Jr." Text of Rosinski's memo appears in this 1965 book of Eccles, pp. 46–47, and is also reproduced in Eccles's *Military Power in a Free Society*, pp. 60–61. For further background on Rosinski's thought see *The Development of Naval Thought: Essays by Herbert Rosinski*, ed. and with an introduction by B. Mitchell Simpson III (Newport, R.I.: Naval War College Press, 1977).

9. The basic early reference is Eccles, "Notes on Strategy as Control: Its Influence on Logistics and Organization" (first draft of working paper prepared under sponsorship of the George Washington University Logistics Research Project, under contract N7 ONR 41904, n.d. [1957]) (EP 82.23).

10. Without minimizing the many contributions of game theory to fundamental strategic analysis, it is important to keep in clear analytic focus substantive issues of logistics, command psychology, and bureaucracy that game theory applications often elide or miss. This task is increasingly important given the numerous civilians in high policy-related roles who are economics trained—training that nowadays widely encourages them to equate "strategic analysis" with game theory.

11. See Eccles, *Military Concepts and Philosophy*, p. 69 (presenting coordinated definitions of strategy, logistics, and tactics as a unified package). As Eccles here defines it, tactics is "the immediate employment of specific forces and weapons to attain strategic objectives"; Eccles's corresponding definition of logistics is reproduced on p. 100 of this article.

12. This three-way distinction builds on Eccles, *Military Power in a Free Society*, p. 70.

13. For a valuable study of basic principles pertaining to general staffs, one that deserves to be much better known today, see Maj. Gen. Otto L. Nelson, Jr., *National Security and the General Staff* (Washington, D.C.: Infantry Journal Press, 1946). Eccles's review in U.S. Naval Institute *Proceedings* 73, no. 6 (June 1947), pp. 720–21, provides a useful, terse introduction to Nelson's massive book. Organizational struggles to surmount "control of the

means of control" problems exist under many other rubrics too (e.g., budget control, surveillance, inspection, internal audit, program evaluation, etc.). As Chinese history can attest, some of these are old—much older, in fact, than the modern general staff.

14. The General Staff Act of 1903 created a general staff for the U.S. Army. It has been commented that by midcentury the United States had acquired, with perhaps characteristically American enthusiasm, *no fewer than ten* kindred entities (military plus civilian Navy staff; ditto, Army; ditto, Air Force; Marine Corps staff; staff of the Office of the Secretary of Defense; National Security Council staff; staff of the Bureau of the Budget, later Office of Management and Budget). Although there were also earlier versions of a joint staff, the Goldwater-Nichols Act of 1986 crystallized what was has been called "a real joint staff." With the early twenty-first century has come Homeland Security, plus the new intelligence bureaucracy.

15. A telling example, from a recent biography of the World War I British Expeditionary Force (BEF) commander in chief, Douglas Haig, is that—in context of a great war on whose outcome the British Empire's fate turned —"Haig could not hope to control *every* aspect of the working of the BEF; *he did not even have complete control over his closest staff*." See Gary Mead, *The Good Soldier: The Biography of Douglas Haig* (London: Atlantic Books, 2007), p. 239 [emphasis supplied].

16. As Eccles noted in 1960: "In modern conflict the man who understands and controls the capabilities and location of electronic command equipment can in effect decide who will wield actual command authority." See Eccles's review of Roland G. Ruppenthal, *Logistical Support of the Armies* (Washington, D.C.: Office of the Chief of Military History, U.S. Army Dept., 1953 and 1959), vol. 2, in *Naval Research Logistics Quarterly* 7, no. 1 (March 1960), p. 97.

17. See Eccles, *Military Power in a Free Society*, p. 56.

18. The case of Saddam Hussein's Iraq comes to mind. See, for example, Jill Crystal, "Authoritarianism and Its Adversaries in the Arab World," *World Politics* 46, no. 2 (January 1994), p. 279.

19. See Robert K. Merton, "Bureaucratic Structure and Personality," *Social Forces* 18, no. 4 (May 1940), p. 563. Pitfalls of goal displacement arising when a strategic situation is changing rapidly may be illustrated by the later stages of some successful coalition wars, when a coalition partner (e.g., the United States as World War II was ending) persists in thinking strategically when it should be thinking *grand strategically*—that is, about how to position for the upcoming postwar situation. Note also the case of post-9/11 U.S. involvement in Afghanistan, whose objectives started with a focus on "Osama Bin Laden dead or alive" and subsequently evolved into versions of nation building there. For some of the complexities of the latter—further illustrating just how difficult the analysis of objectives can be—see Francis Fukuyama, "Nation-Building and the Failure of Institutional Memory," in *Nation-Building: Beyond Afghanistan and Iraq*, ed. Francis Fukuyama (Baltimore: Johns Hopkins Univ. Press, 2006), pp. 1–16.

20. For an illustration of the stresses that thorough analysis of objectives may impose on even a strong coalition, note the difficulties arising in the work of the Anglo-American Combined Chiefs of Staff in World War II—in particular, the challenges faced by Adm. E. J. King and the U.S. Joint Chiefs of Staff "to get the British to commit themselves *in writing.*" See Thomas B. Buell, *Master of Sea Power: A Biography of Fleet Admiral Ernest J. King* (Boston: Little, Brown, 1980), p. 338 [emphasis supplied].

21. As a working approximation, the phrase "traditions of rational choice" refers to majority strands of microeconomics, decision theory, and game theory. Eccles's long-standing intellectual attention to alternatives to rational choice is clear from his analytical work. That attention is well illustrated by Eccles's review in *Naval Research Logistics Quarterly* 10, no. 4 (December 1963), pp. 383–87, of an important work by Karl W. Deutsch, *The Nerves of Government* (New York: Free Press of Glencoe, 1963). For further work along related lines, see Scott A. Boorman, *Alternatives to Rational Choice: Analytical Outline of Substantive Area—Part I*, Preliminary Paper 001013 (New Haven, Conn.: Cowles Foundation, 13 October 2000), and *Alternatives to Rational Choice: Analytical Outline of Substantive Area—Parts II & III*, Preliminary Paper 030116 (New Haven, Conn.: Cowles Foundation, 16 January 2003). Both papers were produced under the auspices of the Cowles Foundation for Research in Economics, Yale University.

22. Eccles's focus on semantic dimensions of strategy, and on language issues more broadly, at times drawing inspiration from Alfred North Whitehead, makes Eccles unusual—indeed, perhaps unique—among logistics-minded analysts of strategy.

23. In this connection, the work translators do merits consideration as an oft-neglected factor in grand strategy. A paper by Eccles analyzes translation problems, among other challenges, facing staff work of the North Atlantic Treaty Organization (NATO) in the crucial formative years of the alliance; see Eccles, "Allied Staffs," U.S. Naval Institute *Proceedings* 79, no. 8 (August 1953), pp. 859–67. Although not usually thought of in this way, reliance on acronyms presents a kind of translation problem, one that at times may also severely hamper clear analysis of objectives.

24. Illustrating some of the possibilities, for certain actors emotions may enter in tie-breaking roles when no uniquely "optimal" course of action presents itself. See, e.g., Jon Elster, "Emotions and Economic Theory," *Journal of Economic Literature* 36, no. 1 (1998), pp. 59–60.

25. It is hard to overstate the extent to which many strategic debates boil down to disagreements over one or another version of the underlying "what kind of war" question (which, of course, was classically posed by Clausewitz: see Carl von Clausewitz, *On War*, ed. and trans. Michael Howard and Peter Paret [Princeton, N.J.: Princeton Univ. Press, 1984], pp. 88–89). An example of a strategic argument pivoting on a "what kind of war" issue is Stephen Biddle, "Seeing Baghdad, Thinking Saigon," *Foreign Affairs* 85, no. 2 (March/April 2006), pp. 2–14.

26. For precisely this reason, the center of gravity of much insightful strategic analysis lies in empirical work "upstream" of the kinds of game-theoretically motivated calculations widely associated with "thinking like a

strategist." For example, shrewd social observation underlies Eccles's sharp-edged
role-playing exercise in strategy in Eccles,
"Allied Staffs," p. 867—beginning, "As a Russian, I would attempt . . ." In this kind of analytic work there remains room for more
sophisticated blending of mathematical and
empirical analytic capabilities (possibly
drawing on some types of social network
analysis).

27. See Eccles, *Military Concepts and Philosophy*,
p. 201. For a larger context see Lyman B.
Kirkpatrick, Jr., "Eccles on Strategy," *Naval
War College Review* 30, no. 1 (Summer 1977),
pp. 10–17.

28. See Martin Shubik, *A Game-Theoretic Approach to Political Economy* (Cambridge,
Mass.: MIT Press, 1984), pp. 643–53. A further relevant direction of analytic work stems
from "garbage can" interpretations of organizational choice. See, e.g., James G. March and
Roger Weissinger-Baylon, eds., *Ambiguity
and Command: Organizational Perspectives on
Military Decision Making* (Marshfield, Mass.:
Pitman, 1986).

29. On the Vietnam War case see Eccles, "The
Vietnam Hurricane," *Shipmate* 36, no. 7
(July–August 1973), pp. 23–26.

30. The potential value of multiple "probes" into
the principles of strategy finds support in
Rear Adm. J. C. Wylie, USN, *Military Strategy: A General Theory of Power Control* (New
Brunswick, N.J.: Rutgers Univ. Press, 1967), a
work also influenced by Rosinski. An en-
larged set of "probes" (seven, not three)—
combining strands of Eccles's and Wylie's
work, along with that of other modern strategic theorists like Capt. Sir Basil H. Liddell
Hart (1895–1970)—is contained in a longer,
unpublished version of the present article.

31. See Eccles's major 1945 report—rich in concrete examples—to Commander, Service
Force, U.S. Pacific Fleet, "The Establishment
of Advanced Naval Bases in the Central Pacific Area, as Seen by the Advanced Base Section, Service Force, U.S. Pacific Fleet," 10
December 1945 (EP 85.2–4; EP 85.3 copy is
further identified as "Collateral Reading for
Correspondence Course in Logistics," Department of Correspondence Courses, U.S.
Naval War College).

32. Already apparent in Eccles's 1947 lecture,
"Basic Elements and Aspects of Logistics," the
distinctively multilevel nature of logistics as a
military concept is further developed in his
"Logistics: What Is It?" *U.S. Naval Institute
Proceedings* 79, no. 6 (June 1953), pp. 645–53
(perhaps Eccles's best-known published paper). For a full-scale, book-length development, see Eccles's *Logistics in the National
Defense*. A Russian perspective on Eccles's
work may be found in a 1963 "pirated" Russian translation of this book containing a detailed analytical preface by a Soviet Navy rear
admiral, V. I. Andreyev (a preface in turn
translated into English by the Office of Naval
Intelligence [EP 11.24]). See EP 64.5 for
translated copy.

33. Illustrating continuing analytic challenges,
see David Moore and Peter D. Antill, "Fo-
cused Logistics: Holy Grail or Poisoned Chal-
ice?" *RUSI Journal* 144, no. 5 (October 1999),
pp. 28–33, itemizing eight potential advan-
tages and ten potential disadvantages of this
concept (also alluding, in a context of disadvantages, to Wylie's theme that "the ultimate
tool of control in war is the man on the scene
with a gun" [*Military Strategy*, p. 87]).

34. The more compact of the two definitions
here is derived from *Pure Logistics*, a pioneering work of Lt. Col. Cyrus Thorpe, USMC,
first published in 1917 and later "rediscov-
ered" and brought to the attention of U.S.
military circles by Eccles. The slightly length-
ier definition crystallized somewhat later but
is thereafter used with high consistency in
Eccles's work—paralleling in this regard his
similarly consistent usage of the term
"strategy."

35. Historical analysis of "dynamics of logistics"
is the focus of two unpublished manuscripts
by Eccles providing some seventy-five pages
of commentary on volumes 1 and 2, respec-
tively, of Ruppenthal, *Logistical Support of the
Armies* (see EP 45.4 and 46.4). A highly condensed version of his commentary on volume
1 appeared in book-review form in U.S. Naval Institute *Proceedings* 80, no. 7 (July 1954),
pp. 813–14. That on volume 2 appeared in
two distinct condensed forms: one book review cited in note 16 above, another in U.S.
Naval Institute *Proceedings* 86, no. 5 (May
1960), pp. 108–11. Dynamic systems aspects
of logistics are further documented in James

A. Huston, *The Sinews of War: Army Logistics, 1775–1953* (Washington, D.C.: Office of the Chief of Military History, U.S. Army, 1966). This work specifically credits Eccles's pioneering analysis of the logistics snowball principle (see p. 659).

36. For military analysis quoting work of Nobel economist Kenneth J. Arrow on trust in a social sense, see Donald Chisholm, "Negotiated Joint Command Relationships: Korean War Amphibious Operations, 1950," *Naval War College Review* 53, no. 2 (Spring 2000), pp. 65–124. Related emphases permeated Eccles's thinking in the 1940s and '50s about many logistics problems. See, e.g., Eccles's discussion of "unnecessary followup" (in context of the requisition system in naval supply depots) in *Logistics in the National Defense*, pp. 187–89. In one of his reviews of Ruppenthal's volume 2, cited in note 35, Eccles writes of the need for "mutual confidence between superior and subordinate," in whose absence the logistics "pendulum can make wide swings between acute shortage, true privation, and reckless overestimates and wastage" (p. 109). Beyond the social trust theme alone, Eccles's analytical work starting in the 1940s allocates substantial attention to "logistic psychology." This topic is approached not merely as a technical area but also as a province of command—epitomized by the struggle to integrate conflicting demands of strategy, logistics, and tactics in the mind of command.

37. Expanding on a related analytical point, Eccles (*Military Power in a Free Society*, p. 63) says: "The word 'logistics' can disappear from all organizational titles and directives, from all curricula, and, in fact, from the military vocabulary itself without in any way influencing the nature of war, the nature of the problem of war, or the problems of command and command decision. The forces of 'military economics' will continue to work regardless of the words and titles used to describe them."

38. Although space does not permit elaboration here, this principle harmonizes with the classic concept of the "indirect approach" to strategy formulated by Capt. Sir Basil H. Liddell Hart (who corresponded with Eccles from the early 1950s until shortly before Liddell Hart's death in 1970).

39. See Eccles, "Pacific Logistics" (presentation, Naval War College, Newport, R.I., 30 March 1946 [delivered while Eccles was serving in Washington as a member of the Joint Operations Review Board]) (EP 30.18). Text of this presentation, along with other analytic writings by Eccles, is cited by Samuel E. Morison, *History of United States Naval Operations in World War II*, vol. 7, *Aleutians, Gilberts and Marshalls, June 1942–April 1944* (Boston: Little, Brown, 1951), p. 100.

40. On 16 February 1991 there was a Scud missile impact in the immediate vicinity of an ammunition-laden pier at Al Jubayl. Importantly, a postwar evaluation observes that "initially, this event received a considerable amount of attention. *However, the initial surge of interest diminished over time* because no personnel injuries and no equipment damage occurred as a result of the missile's impact" [emphasis supplied]. See "Case Narrative: Al Jubayl, Saudi Arabia," Final Report, Special Assistant to the Under Secretary of Defense (Personnel and Readiness) for Gulf War Illnesses, Medical Readiness, and Military Deployments, U.S. Defense Dept., 25 October 2001, available at www.gulflink.osd .mil/al_jub_iii/. Compare historian Alfred W. Crosby's "An Inquiry into the Peculiarities of Human Memory," chap. 15 in *America's Forgotten Pandemic: The Influenza of 1918* (Cambridge, U.K.: Cambridge Univ. Press, 1989), pp. 311–28. Crosby forcefully stresses the puzzling fact that this pandemic was so quickly largely forgotten and had little impact on most organizations and institutions (p. 323). If such collective forgetting could occur in the case of a pandemic that (by Crosby's estimate) in ten months killed more Americans than the "combined battle deaths of personnel of the United States Armed Forces in World War I, World War II, and the Korean and Vietnamese conflicts" (and may have sickened 40 percent of U.S. Navy personnel in 1918), it is reasonable to wonder about the durability in collective memory of lessons in logistics war.

41. Perhaps especially with the fading of World War II memories, it may be easy for American decision makers to become overconfident about the immunity of the superb U.S. logistics capabilities with which they are so familiar. Consider, e.g., David Greenberg,

"Just-in-Time Inventory System Proves Vulnerable to Labor Strife," *Los Angeles Business Journal*, 7 October 2002, p. 13.

42. See Eccles, "Logistics in a Future War" (seminar lecture for Naval Reserve Officers, Third Naval District, U.S. Navy Receiving Station, Brooklyn, N.Y., 18 January 1949 [from which the words quoted in the main text are drawn]) (EP 31.2). See also Eccles's statement, again with an eye to future war, in *Operational Naval Logistics* (p. 151): "Sabotage, in the past never more than a nuisance, may well be serious."

43. Amplifying relevant challenges, Eccles wrote: "*Economic* capabilities limit the combat forces which can be *created*. At the same time, *logistic* capabilities limit the forces which can be *employed* in combat operations" (*Logistics in the National Defense*, p. 41 [emphasis in original]). These two kinds of limitations are clearly intertwined, but they are conceptually distinguishable. Together, they form background to a statement of Robert B. Carney (then vice admiral, USN, and future Chief of Naval Operations): "There you have the meat of the matter: Logistics actually control the Nation's foreign policy by reason of the limiting effect of the Nation's potential in resources." Address to the Naval War College, 12 July 1947, quoted in Eccles, *Operational Naval Logistics*, p. 1.

44. The importance and sheer complexity of never-ending struggles by commanders to exert control over their own logistics is a major theme throughout Eccles's writings. His "logistics snowball" insight emerged as a generalization from logistics experience in World War II in the Pacific, which Eccles knew in great depth. Factors underlying the growth of the snowball are analyzed in his *Logistics in the National Defense*, pp. 102–14. A useful picture of how things have been working quite recently comes from Col. Bradley E. Smith, USA, "The Mandate to Revolutionize Military Logistics," *Air & Space Power Journal* 21, no. 2 (Summer 2007), p. 91: "As *Federal Times* reported on the initial tip of the iceberg, 'During the first month of major combat operations in Iraq two years ago, the Defense Department lost track of $1.2 billion in materials shipped to the Army, encountered hundreds of backlogged shipments, and ran up millions of dollars in fees to lease or replace storage containers because of backlogged or lost shipments.'" See also p. 93 of Colonel Smith's article: "Currently in Iraq, millions of dollars in penalty costs are assessed each month for a multitude of reasons, many of which can be traced back to a fundamental difference of opinion between strategic-level logisticians and tactical-level combat commanders concerning the use of containers. (At the national level, logisticians were leasing and procuring containers as if they were transportation commodities to be quickly returned from Iraq. But tactical-unit commanders did as they always have in combat and held on to containers to be used for mobile storage, bunkers, security walls, and work space.)"

45. Many of the basic problem areas identified by Colonel Smith's 2007 article are reminiscent of problems analyzed forty years earlier by Maj. (later Maj. Gen.) Graham W. Rider, USAF, "Logistics: The Bridge," *Air University Review* 19, no. 1 (November–December 1967), pp. 93–97, whose title is from Eccles's 1959 book. Those problem areas include bureaucracy doing its thing in ways that fail to harmonize logistics efforts across strategic, operational, and tactical levels, a somewhat confused organizational structure, and above all a vital unmet need to integrate information better, all set against a backdrop of failures to apply what we already know—itself a key challenge for logistics education.

46. Working in a supply- and repair-centered context, a pair of RAND Corporation analysts clarify why the quest for improved formulations of basic logistics principles should never cease: While Marine Corps initiatives propose "to reduce the 'iron mountain' using information technology, *some part of that mountain will always remain. . . . Indeed, the smaller the mountain, the more critical it will be to manage it effectively.*" See Ronald D. Fricker, Jr., and Marc L. Robbins, *Retooling for the Logistics Revolution: Designing Marine Corps Inventories to Support the Warfighter* (Santa Monica, Calif.: RAND, 2000), p. xvii [emphasis supplied]. For a classic statement of Eccles's insights into basic logistics principles, see his *Logistics in the National Defense*. Because many of the ideas there reflect Eccles's distinctively integrative, multidisciplinary, logistics background from his

Pacific War experience, Eccles's ideas merit careful study in contexts ranging beyond supply—and perhaps even beyond traditionally recognized logistics functions altogether.

47. Structural forces—many of them essentially bureaucratic—underlying such tendency to diffuseness are analyzed in Eccles, "Logistics," pp. 650–51.

48. A terse, forceful analysis appears in Eccles, "Some Logistics Concepts," *Logistics Spectrum* 11, no. 1 (Spring 1977), pp. 5–8. This paper—importantly anchored in the U.S. logistics experience in Vietnam—was reprinted under the title "How Logistics Systems Behave," *Logistics Spectrum* 16, no. 2 (Summer 1982), pp. 31–34. Eccles's analytical contributions in support of the U.S. naval logistics effort in Vietnam are positively noted by Vice Adm. Edwin Bickford Hooper, USN (Ret.), *Mobility, Support, Endurance: A Story of Naval Operational Logistics in the Vietnam War, 1965–1968* (Washington, D.C.: Naval History Division, U.S. Navy Dept., 1972), p. viii.

49. Text of this 29 September 2008 speech by the secretary of defense is available at www .defenselink.mil/speeches/.

50. Eccles, "Logistics and Strategy" (cited in note 3 above), p. 25; Eccles, *Command Logistics*, p. 8.

51. See, e.g., Eccles, *Military Concepts and Philosophy*, p. 48.

52. An example of a challenging problem of self-control—involving the inner circle of high command at the height of a major crisis—is the case, during the 1962 Cuban missile crisis, of the Executive Committee, whose fifteen members sought to preserve the secrecy of key impending U.S. strategic steps by, for example, keeping "routine appointments where possible." See Theodore C. Sorensen, *Kennedy* (New York: Harper and Row, 1965), p. 698.

53. For an illustration of strategic thinking aiming to look more than a human generation ahead—the context being an estimate of how long communism was likely to survive before, in Eccles's words, "failing under its own faults"—see Eccles, "The World Outlook of Communism (a Comparison between Communist Philosophy and American Philosophy)" (seminar lecture for Naval Reserve Officers, Third Naval District, U.S. Navy Receiving Station, Brooklyn, 19 October 1948) (EP 29.2). Counting in slightly different units, it is said of Bismarck that he thought in terms of the war after next.

54. A related acronym in current circulation is DIME ("diplomacy, information, military, and economics"). One pitfall with any such acronym, of course, is that it may encourage thinking to stop with the received categories. Such a stopping rule may work at some lower levels of action but not in true grand strategy—where opportunities may arise from being early to recognize and exploit some coherent, perhaps emerging, set of tools that is not "one to one" with any of the given categories and may in important respects scramble them. (It is also worth noting that an online source, Acronymfinder.com, last visited 11 October 2008, identifies no fewer than fourteen other meanings of "DIME"—some slightly different from that just given, others very different.)

55. In the background stands the timeless challenge of achieving genuine integration of planning and decision processes. This is a problem, having both specifically military and wider strategic facets, where Eccles's strategic thinking provides much valuable insight, building in part on his Joint Operations Review Board background mentioned in note 39; his 1951–52 role, in a challenging period early in NATO's history, as Assistant Chief of Staff, Logistics, for Commander, Allied Forces Southern Europe (CINCSOUTH); plus relevant analytical work (see, e.g., Eccles, *Logistics in the National Defense*, pp. 79–101).

56. Well after the events of 9/11, a basic related problem—one whose impact permeates the U.S. defense establishment from a grand-strategic down to a tactical level—remains continuing insufficiency of personnel with appropriate capabilities in critical languages. See, e.g., Will Bardenwerper, "For Military, Slow Progress in Foreign Language Push: Struggle Persists over a Training Objective," *New York Times*, 22 September 2008, p. A20.

57. Note a French army officer's well informed account, based on his command experience as a junior officer in France's Algerian war, of two contrasting mentalities in counterinsurgency warfare—whose exemplars he terms "warriors" and "psychologists." See David

Galula, *Pacification in Algeria, 1956–1958*, with new foreword by Bruce Hoffman (Santa Monica, Calif.: RAND, 2006), pp. 64–68. To the extent that doctrine can help bridge diverse mentalities, one idea—inspired in part by work with the Eccles Papers, in part by recent advances in network analysis—is "seeding" carefully chosen imaginative cross-references to connect doctrine statements whose subject matters would usually be regarded as unrelated or largely so. The goal of doing so would be to help encourage disciplined but creative intellectual cross-fertilization and analogical thinking.

58. A particularly forceful—in part because it is so very terse—comment by Eccles directed against weapon strategy stands the test of time so well as to merit quotation here: "A great danger lies in the possible domination of strategy by weapons rather than by national objectives. National objectives ultimately are developed by the aspirations, character, and sense of values of the people, not by a technological triumph.

"If one becomes committed to a strategy which is based on a weapon rather than upon national objectives, a sense of frustration is bound to ensue. *Frustration frequently leads men of high spirit to commit acts of reckless irresponsibility*" (Eccles, "The Great Debate," U.S. Naval Institute *Proceedings* 80, no. 7 [July 1954], p. 809, [emphasis supplied]). The context for these words was, of course, nuclear weapons and strategic airpower; the substance could extend to other weapons systems—or to systems or capabilities of other kinds, civilian as well as military.

59. Certain relevant military possibilities, importantly including possibilities of algorithm sabotage suggested by a (nonsabotage) naval warfare example from the 1982 Falklands War, are analyzed in Scott A. Boorman and Paul R. Levitt, "Deadly Bugs," *Chicago Tribune Magazine*, 3 May 1987, p. 19ff. See also Scott A. Boorman and Paul R. Levitt, "Software Warfare and Algorithm Sabotage," *Signal* 42, no. 9 (May 1988), p. 75ff.

60. See Tami Davis Biddle, *Rhetoric and Reality in Air Warfare: The Evolution of British and American Ideas about Strategic Bombing, 1914–1945* (Princeton, N.J.: Princeton Univ. Press, 2002), especially the discussion of the "industrial fabric theory" on pp. 163, 296–97.

61. In fact, al-Qa'ida "strategy" invites thorough critical analysis along related lines. A key (if perhaps long-term) limitation, and possibly exploitable vulnerability, of al-Qa'ida may grow out of its apparent basic preoccupation with strategy-as-destruction rather than strategy-as-control.

62. Illustrating some of the intellectual possibilities, Karl W. Deutsch noted ancient Parthian modes of warfare involving attacks directed "at first not so much against the principal material resources but rather against the decision-making capacity" of an adversary. See *Nerves of Government*, pp. 62, 274–75; Eccles, "Strategy: The Essence of Professionalism," *Naval War College Review* 24, no. 4 (December 1971), p. 50.

63. See Thomas C. Schelling, *The Strategy of Conflict* (Cambridge, Mass.: Harvard Univ. Press, 1960), p. 36ff., and his *Arms and Influence* (New Haven, Conn.: Yale Univ. Press, 1966), p. 35–91.

64. See Morison, *Aleutians, Gilberts and Marshalls, June 1942–April 1944*, pp. 100–13. Still an important source, by virtue of its author's key pioneering role in wartime creation of a mobile logistics support capability, is Rear Adm. Worrall R. Carter, USN (Ret.), *Beans, Bullets, and Black Oil* (Washington, D.C.: U.S. Government Printing Office, 1953).

65. Consider Mao Zedong as strategist of revolution versus the Mao who later led the People's Republic of China into the Great Leap Forward and the Cultural Revolution.

66. The relevant spirit of strategy/logistics synthesis is captured by former Chief of Naval Operations (CNO) Adm. Robert B. Carney, USN (Ret.): "Some General Observations and Experiences in Logistics," *Naval Research Logistics Quarterly* 3, nos. 1 and 2 (March–June 1956), pp. 1–9 (building in part on Carney's World War II background as Adm. William Halsey's chief of staff, plus his postwar role as Deputy CNO for Logistics).

67. A good set of approaches to all three tasks should be crafted to meet the needs of both *strategic planners* and *strategic analysts*—two different roles that are often confused. The crux of the difference is clarified by Eccles, *Military Concepts and Philosophy*, p. 44: "A strategic analyst can contribute greatly to the

understanding of strategy without necessarily being qualified to originate and develop a specific national or military strategy. On the other hand, there have been excellent strategists who have not made major contributions to the historical or theoretical analysis of strategy. For example, the maxims of Napoleon were gleaned from his notes and letters, while Admiral Spruance has never written any comprehensive statement of his own concepts of strategy."

68. The spirit of a counterpart in strategic studies to the "endless frontier" of science concept of Vannevar Bush is captured by an unpublished Eccles document, "Control of the Sea": "No single person can ever say everything about control of the sea nor should we expect agreement in all that is said by competent authority. Nevertheless, from time to time deep thinkers will express their thoughts on fundamental truths with such insight and clarity that their words should be carefully preserved and repeatedly referred to. A specific example of this is contained in Admiral Spruance's discussion of control of the sea. The excellent expressions of fundamental truth should not be considered as a rigid and final formulation but rather as a sound basis upon which men can establish their own line of thinking and ideas. The development of further ideas on this basis is important and many novel interpretations and expressions can be usefully developed. However, the search for novelty and fresh formulations should not go on without periodic reference back to the classic thought." A copy bearing the dates 25 October 1956 and 14 December 1965 is in EP 82.23 in the Eccles Papers.

CPSIA information can be obtained at www.ICGtesting.com
Printed in the USA
BVOW09s0225150615

404635BV00005B/28/P